This Is the Feast

Preparing for the Lord's Supper

Student Book

Dean Nadasdy and Thomas Doyle

CONCORDIA PUBLISHING HOUSE • SAINT LOUIS

Contents

© 2015 Concordia Publishing House
3558 S. Jefferson Avenue, St. Louis, MO 63118-3968
1-800-325-3040 • cph.org

All rights reserved. No part of this publication may be reproduced, stored in a retrieval system, or transmitted, in any form or by any means, electronic, mechanical, photocopying, recording, or otherwise, without the prior written permission of Concordia Publishing House.

Edited by Rodney L. Rathmann

Artwork © Concordia Publishing House

Scripture quotations are from the ESV® Bible (The Holy Bible, English Standard Version®), copyright © 2001 by Crossway, a publishing ministry of Good News Publishers. Used by permission. All rights reserved.

Hymnal quotations with the abbreviation *LSB* are from *Lutheran Service Book*, copyright © 2006 Concordia Publishing House. All rights reserved.

5 6 7 8 9 10 11 12 13 32 31 30 29 28 27 26 25 24

Session 1

The Law and Giving Myself a Test

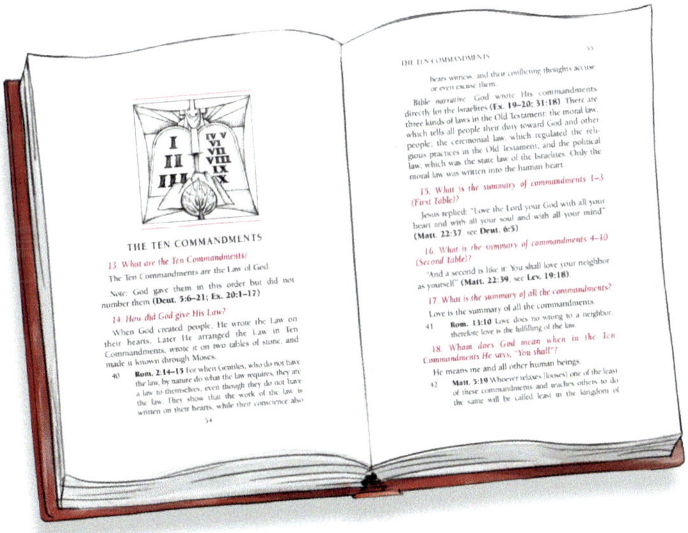

Key Verse

Let a person examine himself, then, and so eat of the bread and drink of the cup. 1 Corinthians 11:28

Drama

If Mirrors Could Talk

(NARRATOR [N] stands Stage R. Three players [M1, M2, M3] stand Stage L, facing the audience, each holding a large mirror. GIRL stands Center Stage.)

N: Once there was a girl who had three mirrors. These were not ordinary mirrors. These mirrors talked. The girl loved the mirrors because they always said something that made her feel good. When she didn't like how she looked, she went to her first mirror and asked,

GIRL: *(Moves to M1; stands in front of it)* Tell me, mirror, what do you see?

M1: I see a very pretty person.

GIRL: Pretty, you say?

M1: The prettiest of all.

N: And the girl smiled, thinking herself to be the prettiest girl of all. *(Girl moves to M2, standing in front of it.)* When the girl was feeling very guilty about having done something wrong, she said,

GIRL: I feel terrible. I shouldn't have done it.

N: And she looked into her second mirror with all her guilt, and the mirror said,

M2: Don't feel bad. You're a good person.

GIRL: Good, you say?

M2: The very best of all.

N: And the girl smiled, thinking herself to be very good, even though she had done something bad. *(GIRL moves to M3, standing in front of it.)* When the girl doubted herself, when she wondered if she could do what she had to do, she thought,

GIRL: I don't think I can do this. I am too weak. I'll never be able to do it.

N: She looked into her third mirror with all her doubt, and the mirror said,

M3: Yes, you can. You can do it. You're strong.

GIRL: Strong, you say?

M3: The strongest of all.

N: The girl loved her mirrors, all right. They made her feel pretty and good and strong. Yet something inside of her made her wonder if she could trust these mirrors that always told her what she wanted to hear. *(GIRL moves to M1.)*

M1: The prettiest. *(GIRL moves to M2.)*

M2: The best. *(GIRL moves to M3.)*

M3: The strongest.

N: She wondered about the mirrors that talked and if they could be trusted.

Discuss:

1. Why do you think the girl loved her mirrors?
2. Why do you think she wondered if they could be trusted?
3. What's wrong with only looking at the good in us and never seeing the bad?
4. How do you know if you've done something wrong?

Looking for Answers

1. Describe the three ways the Law of God functions in our lives. How is each important?

   Curb—1 Timothy 1:9

   Mirror—Romans 3:20

   Rule—Psalm 119:105

2. Because God is holy and just, what does He require of every person? Read Matthew 5:48. How well have you lived up to God's standard?

3. If honest, what must we confess? See 1 John 1:8.

4. What do we deserve because of our sin? Read Romans 6:23.

5. What does God teach us in His Word concerning sin?

   a. 1 John 3:4

   b. Psalm 51:5

   c. Romans 8:7

   d. Galatians 5:19–21

6. Why is using the Law as a mirror so important as we prepare to receive the Lord's Supper?

7. What does using the Law as a mirror show me about myself?

8. What do you conclude about yourself as you look into the mirror of God's Law?

9. Considering your conclusion, why is it important for you to receive the Lord's Supper? See Matthew 26:26–28.

What Do You See?

1. What elements of this work of art indicate God's presence? See also Exodus 19:17–19.

2. What emotion are the people expressing in this picture? See Exodus 20:18.

3. Note the position of Moses in the picture, standing as the intermediary between God and His people. How does Moses in this picture remind us of Jesus?

The Ten Commandments

Taking It Home

Spend at least 10 minutes discussing with a parent the following questions:

1. How is God's Law important to you?
2. How do you prepare for the Lord's Supper?
3. What do you receive from God when you eat His body and drink His blood in the Lord's Supper?
4. Share a time when going to the Lord's Supper was especially important to you.

Grace and the Gospel

Key Verse

Therefore, since we have been justified by faith, we have peace with God through our Lord Jesus Christ. Romans 5:1

Drama

On Being Found

(NARRATOR [N] stands Stage R; BOY with nicely decorated gift box [with envelope and letter inside] stands Center Stage. DAD stands Stage L.)

N: Once there was a boy who found a large box in his attic.

BOY: *(Holding box)* Wow! Now, this is really something! *(Shakes box and listens to determine what might be inside.)*

N: Actually, the box sort of found him. Reaching high onto a shelf for an old baseball bat, he had knocked down both the bat and the box, and both had fallen right on his head.

BOY: *(Feels top of his head)* Wow! I can still feel it.

N: The box was beautifully wrapped in paper that looked very old. The box was very light, and the boy clearly had one thing on his mind.

BOY: *(Shakes box again and listens)* Wow! Gotta find out what's inside. *(Moves to DAD at Stage L)*

N: So the boy went to his dad and said,

BOY: Dad, look what I found!

DAD: How did you find that?

BOY: *(Rubbing head)* Well, it sort of found me. What do you know about this, Dad?

DAD: I know it was left for you.

BOY: Really? By whom?

DAD: By my grandfather, your great-grandfather. He told me to save it for you, for when you were old enough to appreciate it.

BOY: So?

DAD: So what?

BOY: So, am I old enough?

DAD: I think so. Go ahead and open it.

BOY: Wow! Okay! *(Tears through wrappings, opens box, digs through old newspapers to find an envelope)* An envelope! It says, "To my great-grandchild."

DAD: Go ahead. Open it. *(BOY opens envelope, takes letter from envelope.)* What does it say?

BOY: It says . . .

DAD: Go ahead and read it, Son.

BOY: To my great-grandchild. You don't know me, but I am your great-grandfather. I died before you were born. But I asked your father to put this away and give it to you when you were old enough to appreciate it. I want you to know who you are and where you came from . . .

N: And the boy continued to read. He found out much about himself and his family—that his great-grandfather had worked seven years as a servant to raise the money to come to America. He learned that his great-grandfather was the first in his family ever to finish college. He learned that an inheritance had been set aside for him.

BOY: An inheritance? Can you believe this?

N: He learned that his great-grandfather had been a man of strong Christian faith who wanted his family to be rich in faith as well. All the boy could say was,

BOY: Can you believe this? I never knew!

N: He kept the letter. He called it his good-news letter. He was thankful for the day he found it, or, rather, the day when it found him. And when he needed to remember who he was and where he had come from, where he belonged and what he believed, he took out that good-news letter. He read it aloud again and again, and said,

BOY: Can you believe this?

Discuss:

1. How is *grace*—an undeserved gift—evident in this story?
2. How is the great-grandfather's letter like the Bible?
3. Why did the boy keep saying, "Can you believe this?"
4. How are we like the boy when we remember what Jesus did for us on the cross?

Looking for Answers

1. More than anything else, what does God's Law show us about ourselves? See Romans 3:20–24.

2. Grace describes God's undeserved gift of forgiveness for sins and eternal life through faith in Jesus' death on the cross.

   a. What does God's grace tell us about God?

   b. What does God's grace tell us about ourselves?

3. How does God describe His grace?

   a. Romans 3:24

   b. Romans 5:8

   c. Ephesians 1:7

4. The Gospel is the Good News that we are freed from the guilt, the punishment, and the power of sin and are saved eternally from our sin because of Christ keeping the Law and suffering and dying on the cross for us. How is God's grace demonstrated in the Gospel?

5. When we receive the Lord's Supper, we "proclaim the Lord's death until He comes" (1 Corinthians 11:26). Why did Jesus have to die? How did God demonstrate His grace in Jesus' death? How is Jesus' death Good News?

6. The Bible uses many words to help us understand what God has accomplished for us by grace in Jesus Christ. Three of these appear in Romans 3:23–26. Read these verses. Then describe briefly what is meant by each word.

   a. Justified

   b. Redemption

   c. Propitiation

7. The boy in the play exclaimed enthusiastically, "Can you believe this?" In the Apostles' and Nicene Creeds, we confess enthusiastically, "I believe . . . ." Why?

What Do You See?

1. Describe the human emotion portrayed in this work of art.
2. What does Jesus' suffering have to do with you?
3. Explain the concept of God's grace for us as illustrated in this picture.

With His holy, precious blood and with His innocent suffering and death

Taking It Home

Spend at least 10 minutes with a parent talking about the following:

1. When in our lives have we experienced the grace of God in a special way?
2. What do Christians mean when they confess in the Apostles' and Nicene Creeds, "I believe . . ."?
3. Jesus said "Remember Me" when He instituted the Lord's Supper. What do you especially remember about Jesus when you come to Communion?

Session 3

How God Gives Me Gifts

Key Verse

For in Christ Jesus you are all sons of God, through faith. For as many of you as were baptized into Christ have put on Christ. Galatians 3:26–27

Drama

Come, Lord Jesus

(MOM, DAD, JEFF, and ANN sit Center Stage at a table, facing the audience. The table may be set for dinner.)

DAD: Doesn't this look great? So who would like to say grace?

ANN: Let us pray. *(ALL bow heads.)* Bless this food, Lord, and bless our family. Thanks for the love we share and for the new TV You're going to give us. Now hear us as we pray.

JEFF: Way to go, Annie. I like that part about the TV.

DAD: You want to tell us about that?

MOM: Yes, Annie, please. I didn't know we were looking for a new TV.

ANN: Are you kidding, Mom? Have you seen the picture lately? And we only have a 32-inch screen. Everybody I know has at least a 50-inch flat screen.

JEFF: Little Annie here knows her TV screens.

MOM: So you thought you'd mention it in your prayer? You thought you'd thank God for it before you even had it?

ANN: I just thought that if I got God listening . . .

JEFF: He might start making things happen. I like that!

ANN: Which makes me wonder, Mom and Dad—why do we always say, "Come, Lord Jesus"?

DAD: You're changing the subject, Annie.

ANN: No, really; doesn't Jesus come anyway? Isn't He "where two . . ."—how does it go?

JEFF: "Where two or three are gathered."

ANN: Yeah, that's it. Doesn't He just come to every meal?

MOM: He does, but we say "Come, Lord Jesus" to let Him know how much we love Him, how much we'd be honored to have Him join us again.

DAD: Sort of like when we pray, "Thy kingdom come." He comes without our prayer, but we want Him to know that we'd be thrilled to have Him come right among us.

JEFF: Like in church, with the sermon. He comes there.

ANN: And the Lord's Supper. He comes there too.

DAD: Exactly.

ANN: So what about TVs? What about 50-inch screens?

MOM: That may be another story, young lady.

DAD: We'll have to leave that one to God.

JEFF: You gotta admit, though, it was a nice try.

Discuss:

1. Why do meals and prayers seem to go together in so many families?
2. What does saying the "Come, Lord Jesus" prayer before a meal mean to you?

Looking for Answers

1. How does God offer the gift of His forgiveness?

   a. Romans 1:16

   b. John 3:16

   c. Ephesians 1:7

2. The written and spoken Word of the Gospel and the Sacraments are the Means of Grace.

   a. How does the Bible describe the spoken and written Word of God? Read Luke 24:27 and 2 Timothy 3:16–17.

   b. How does the Bible describe the Sacraments? Read Acts 2:38 and 1 Corinthians 10:16.

3. What does God provide to us in His Sacraments?

   a. Acts 22:16

   b. Matthew 26:28

4. Besides forgiveness, what other blessings does God give us in Baptism?

   a. Titus 3:5

   b. John 3:5

   c. Romans 6:4

   d. Galatians 3:26

   e. 1 John 3:1

5. When Jesus began (instituted) the Lord's Supper, He was celebrating the Passover meal with His disciples.

   a. What did people remember when they celebrated the Passover? Skim Exodus 12–14.

   b. What do we remember when we receive the Lord's Supper? Read 1 Corinthians 11:26.

6. Compare and contrast the Passover meal and the Lord's Supper.

What Do You See?

1. How do the images down the center of the picture connect with the names we use when someone is baptized?

2. Describe the expressions on the people's faces. What does this say about Baptism?

The Baptism of Jesus

Taking It Home

Spend at least 10 minutes with a parent discussing the following questions.

1. What family traditions do we have to celebrate holidays and special days?
2. What do you remember about my Baptism day?
3. What does it mean to you when you receive the Lord's Supper?
4. How does the Lord's Supper strengthen us as a family?

Before the next session, review the questions and answers from the Sacrament of Holy Baptism section of *Luther's Small Catechism with Explanation*.

Session 4

Real Presence

Key Verse

Now as they were eating, Jesus took bread, and after blessing it broke it and gave it to the disciples, and said, "Take, eat; this is My body." And He took a cup, and when He had given thanks He gave it to them, saying, "Drink of it, all of you, for this is My blood of the covenant, which is poured out for many for the forgiveness of sins." Matthew 26:26–28

Drama

The President's Presence

(JOEL is at Stage R near a stand or podium on which sits a large picture of the current president of the United States. MOLLY and JON are at Stage L. JON holds an invitation; one or both may have a camera. NARRATOR [N] may step in and out of the scene.)

MOLLY: I can't believe this! Read it again, Jon.

JON: You know it by heart, Molly. You got an invitation too.

MOLLY: Just read it. I love the sound of it.

JON: You are herewith cordially invited to spend a day with the President of the United States. He will be present with you from ten o'clock in the morning at the residence of Joel Schmidt. Please arrive promptly at ten for a day in the President's presence. Signed, THE WHITE HOUSE.

MOLLY: That's the part I like best—"a day in the President's presence." What time is it?

JON: Nine thirty.

MOLLY: We should probably head over.

JON: How Joel pulled this off I'll never know, but let's go.

N: Imagine an invitation like that! Wow, to spend a day in the president's presence! That's what Molly and Jon look forward to, but let's see what really happens. *(MOLLY and JON approach Stage R and stand as if at a door.)*

JON: *(Ready to ring doorbell)* Well, here goes.

MOLLY: Shouldn't there be security or something?

JON: Probably on the inside. Here goes. *(Mimes pressing doorbell; NARRATOR makes sound of doorbell.)*

JOEL: *(Mimes opening door)* You made it.

JON: We wouldn't have missed it.

JOEL: Well, come on in.

MOLLY: When does he arrive? The invitation said ten o'clock. I know we're a little early.

JOEL: Oh, he's here already.

JON: *(Doubtfully)* Really? Where?

JOEL: *(Returns to stand by picture and motions to it)* You're looking at him. *(Proudly, as if introducing him)* The President of the United States!

MOLLY: But that's not the president. It's just a picture.

JON: The invitation said we would spend a day in the president's presence.

JOEL: Right. Here he is.

MOLLY: But it's not the president, not really. It's not real. How can we ask any questions?

JOEL: *(Frustrated and holding up camera)* And who wants a picture of a picture?

MOLLY: It isn't the same, Joel. It just isn't the same.

N: It isn't the same, you know. A picture is not a presence.

Discuss:

1. For whose presence are you especially grateful today? In other words, who makes you very glad because he or she is more than a picture?
2. How is having a picture different from having a real person?
3. What does it mean to you to know that Jesus is really present in the Lord's Supper?
4. How is that different from Him just being represented by the bread and wine?

Looking for Answers

1. What are four names for Holy Communion? What do these names mean to you?

   a. 1 Corinthians 10:16

   b. 1 Corinthians 11:20

   c. 1 Corinthians 10:21

   d. Acts 2:42

2. What did Jesus say when He distributed the bread to His disciples? See Matthew 26:26.

3. What did Jesus say when He distributed the wine to His disciples? See Matthew 26:28.

4. What did Jesus mean when He said, "This is My body. . . . This is My blood"? Read 1 Corinthians 10:16 and also 11:27–29.

5. What do we still receive when we eat His body and drink His blood? What do we still receive when we eat bread and drink wine in the Lord's Supper? Read 1 Corinthians 10:16.

6. We call this miracle "real presence." Jesus' body and blood are really present in, with, and under the bread and wine. How do we respond as we come into the real presence of Jesus in the Lord's Supper? (Consider the play read earlier.)

What Do You See?

1. What attitudes about the Lord's Supper does the artist express in the picture?

2. What might be the artist's intended message in focusing the disciples' gaze on the cup Jesus holds?

3. Look at the bread centered on the table. What does it foreshadow?

The Lord's Supper

Taking It Home

Spend at least 10 minutes with a parent discussing the following questions:

1. Whose real, live presence do you especially appreciate?

2. What do you think and feel as you come into the real presence of Jesus in the Lord's Supper?

Before the next session, review together the questions and answers from the Sacrament of the Altar portion of *Luther's Small Catechism with Explanation.*

Meal of Forgiveness

Key Verse

For by a single offering He has perfected for all time those who are being sanctified. Hebrews 10:14

Drama

Guilt Free

(NARRATOR [N] at Stage R. GIRL and GUILT at Stage L. GUILT [perhaps dressed in black] stands directly behind GIRL and follows right behind her wherever she goes. FRIEND is offstage.)

N: Once there was a girl who was very guilty. *(GIRL begins to walk about; GUILT follows right at her back.)* Wherever she went, her guilt went with her.

GIRL: Oh, I know I shouldn't have done it. I was very wrong.

GUILT: *(In GIRL's ear)* You sure were. You were as wrong as wrong can be.

GIRL: So what do I do now? *(Stops walking about)*

GUILT: You live with it.

GIRL: It?

GUILT: You live with me, your guilt. You're stuck with me. Where you go, I go.

GIRL: *(Walks again; GUILT follows on her heels.)* I hate you.

GUILT: No, you hate yourself. I wouldn't be here if you hadn't done it.

GIRL: I know. You're right, of course. *(Still pacing, with GUILT following)* Maybe I should read a book. You know, one of those self-help books that will tell me I'm really just fine.

GUILT: I'll still be here. The kind of book you're after will never get the best of me.

GIRL: Well then, I'll just forget about it. That's it. I'll deny it.

GUILT: Won't work. I'll be on your back lickety-split.

GIRL: Lickety-split?

GUILT: I won't let you forget.

N: It isn't easy getting rid of guilt.

GIRL: I'll phone Susie. I love Susie. She'll tell me that it's okay and not to worry.

GUILT: I'll tell you that you can't trust Susie, that it's not okay, and that you're really a bad person.

GIRL: *(Stops with GUILT right at her back)* Then what happens next? Do I live forever with you on my back?

N: And that's exactly what she would have done—lived with her guilt forever—if someone had not come. *(FRIEND enters Stage L and walks up to GUILT.)* One who was stronger and greater than she. One who looked guilt in the eye and said,

FRIEND: Get behind me. You're mine now.

N: And sure enough *(GUILT steps behind FRIEND)*, the girl's guilt became his, and as he walked away *(FRIEND exits Stage L with GUILT at his back)*, he said with a face-wide smile,

FRIEND: You're free of guilt now. I'm taking it away. *(FRIEND and GUILT exit.)*

N: The girl stood still and looked over her shoulder, and she smiled too and said,

GIRL: I am guilt free. *(Smiles and walks off confidently)*

Discuss:

1. In what way is the girl like us when we've sinned?
2. What bad ways of handling guilt was the girl going to try?
3. How is Jesus a friend to sinners when considering our guilt?

Looking for Answers

1. What is the chief blessing of Holy Communion? See Matthew 26:28.
2. Before Jesus died on the cross, the Jewish priests sacrificed animals daily for the forgiveness of sins. How is Jesus' sacrifice on the cross different from and better than these other sacrifices? See Hebrews 10:10–12.
3. When we celebrate the Lord's Supper, is Christ sacrificed over and over again each time? See Hebrews 10:14, 18.
4. How do you know for sure that your sins are forgiven in the Lord's Supper? See Matthew 26:28 and 1 John 1:7.
5. What other blessings does God provide in the Lord's Supper? Read Romans 6:8–9 and 1 Peter 2:24.
6. Consider how guilt followed the girl around in the play read earlier. Now read what God says about our sins forgiven through faith in Jesus' death on the cross. Read Psalm 103:12. How can you respond as guilt tries to follow you around, reminding you of past sins?

What Do You See?

1. Contrast the appearance of the son with the appearance of the father. What can this tell you about yourself and your relationship with the heavenly Father?

2. The father reaches out to welcome and embrace the returning son. How is this like God when we return to Him seeking forgiveness?

Jesus Seeks the Lost

Taking It Home

Spend 10 minutes or more discussing the following questions with your parent(s):

1. When did we last share a word of forgiveness between us?
2. What makes forgiving someone so difficult sometimes?
3. What do we think about when we pray "Forgive us our trespasses as we forgive those who trespass against us"?
4. What do I think and feel when I look at a cross and consider that Jesus sacrificed His life for me?

Before the next session, review the questions and answers from the Sacrament of the Altar section of *Luther's Small Catechism with Explanation.*

Other Blessings Received in Holy Communion

Key Verse

The cup of blessing that we bless, is it not a participation in the blood of Christ? The bread that we break, is it not a participation in the body of Christ? Because there is one bread, we who are many are one body, for we all partake of the one bread. 1 Corinthians 10:16–17

Drama

A Dinner Not Soon Forgotten

(ALL at Center Stage; MOM to the right of MARY and LISA)

MARY: So what was it like?

LISA: I'll never forget it.

MARY: I think you're the first person I've ever met who actually won a contest. Just think of it—dinner with him!

LISA: And I didn't even do anything to win.

MOM: Sure you did, Lisa. You filled out the entry card and dropped it in the box.

LISA: Wow, some real talent there. I mean, I didn't have to sing or write an essay or anything.

MOM: But you did win.

LISA: Someone drew my name out of a box.

MARY: Yes, a box with the names of thousands of other kids who wanted to have dinner with him. So are you going to tell me about it or not?

MOM: Tell her, Lisa.

MARY: What's he like?

LISA: He's everything I thought he would be—kind, funny, smart.

MARY: And handsome.

LISA: That too.

MARY: What did he say?

LISA: We talked about all kinds of things, mostly about me.

MARY: About you? He talked about you?

LISA: He asked questions, almost like he was interested in me—as a person, I mean.

MARY: *(Swooning)* Wow-w-w. So what did he ask?

LISA: About my family, our school, my friends, what I want to do when I grow up.

MARY: And you answered him? You talked to him?

LISA: No, I sat there slurping soup. Yes, I answered him.

MARY: Wow-w-w. What did you say?

LISA: A lot of things. Mostly "thanks," though. I think I must have said "thanks" ten thousand times. I mean, like, he was having dinner with me! It's something I'll never forget. I felt like I was there with every girl my age. He knew how I felt.

MARY: And when you said "thanks," what did he say?

LISA: He said, "You're welcome."

MARY: Wow-w-w. Wow-w-w.

Discuss:

1. With whom do you think Lisa had dinner? Explain your response.
2. How is dinner with someone special similar to Holy Communion?

Looking for Answers

1. Besides forgiveness, life, and salvation, what other blessings does God give you in Holy Communion? Read Romans 8:10 and 1 Corinthians 10:17.
2. Read 1 Corinthians 11:26 and answer these questions:
   a. What event will you proclaim or announce when you come to Holy Communion?
   b. What event will you most look forward to when you come to Holy Communion?
3. Read 1 Corinthians 10:16–17. Diagram the circles of belonging—unity—in which Christians participate when they receive the Lord's Supper.
4. In what ways will the Lord strengthen you in the Lord's Supper? See 1 Peter 2:24.
5. In what way(s) is Communion a meal of thanksgiving?

What Do You See?

1. Describe the people receiving Holy Communion in this picture. What message is this illustration seeking to convey?

2. Explain the significance of going to the altar to receive the very body and blood of Jesus for the forgiveness of sins.

3. Note the cross on the altar. Where is the focus when we receive the Lord's Supper? Why?

The Sacrament of the Altar

Taking It Home

Spend 10 minutes or more discussing the following questions with your parent(s):

1. How is the unity you celebrate in the Lord's Supper important to you?
2. Who comes to mind when you hear the words "and with all the company of heaven"? Whom do you love in heaven who is praising God?
3. In your own words, try to answer someone who asks, "What's so special about Communion in your church?"

Before the next session, memorize 1 Corinthians 10:16–17.

Table Graces

Key Verse

You prepare a table before me in the presence of my enemies; You anoint my head with oil; my cup overflows. Surely goodness and mercy shall follow me all the days of my life, and I shall dwell in the house of the LORD forever. Psalm 23:5–6

Drama

Setting the Table

(MOM's voice is heard offstage. JAMIE is setting a table at Center Stage. A table with tablecloth and appropriate utensils may be used, or JAMIE may mime the action without props.)

MOM: Jamie, do you want to try setting the table?

JAMIE: *(Setting plates)* I am trying to set the table, Mom. Emily Toast would be proud of me.

MOM: That's "Post," sweetie. Emily Post.

JAMIE: Right. *(To audience)* Emily Toast is some expert on etiquette my mom is always talking about. We're having a big dinner tonight. My brother's coming home after four years in the Air Force.

MOM: Two forks on the left, Jamie . . .

JAMIE: *(Setting silverware)* Knife and spoon on the right. Gotcha, Mom.

MOM: Spoon on the outside . . .

JAMIE: Salad fork on the outside left. Under control. *(Sarcastically)* Travis will appreciate it. *(To audience)* Travis is the flyboy home for good. Actually, I don't know if he'll even notice the silverware.

MOM: Yes, he will, Jamie. That's his great-grandmother's good china, and he knows it only gets used for the finest occasions. You set for how many?

JAMIE: *(Kiddingly)* Three hundred. Right, Mom?

MOM: Jamie.

JAMIE: It's set for eight *(counting)*—the four of us, Grandpa, Ellie, Pastor, and Mrs. Tyler. *(To audience)* "The four of us!" I like the sound of that. Mom, Dad, Travis, and me! Ellie is Travis's fiancée. Grandpa wouldn't miss this dinner. And Mom thought it would be nice to have Pastor here too. *(Setting wine and water crystal on table)* My great-grandmother brought this china and crystal over from Europe.

MOM: Use the best crystal.

JAMIE: Nothing but the finest. *(Places napkins in water glasses; stands in silence, admiring the table)*

MOM: *(Enters Stage R with floral centerpiece; places it on table)* And this! *(Joins JAMIE in a long look at the table)* Right, Jamie. Nothing but the finest for Travis. Home at last, safe and sound.

JAMIE: It will be good to have us all together again.

MOM: Like Grandma used to say . . .

JAMIE: *(To audience)* The one who had the china . . .

MOM: My cup runneth over!

Discuss:

1. How is the meal in the drama like the Lord's Supper?
2. Where in the Church's celebration of Communion do you see "nothing but the finest" at work?

Looking for Answers

1. Why is it so important to have bread and wine for the celebration of the Lord's Supper? See Matthew 26:26–28 and Luke 22:14–20.

2. Who is worthy to receive the Lord's Supper? See 1 Corinthians 11:27–29.

3. How are we to examine ourselves before receiving the Lord's Supper?

   a. Psalm 38:18

   b. 2 Corinthians 13:5

   c. Ephesians 4:22–24

4. Can I receive the Lord's Supper when my faith is weak? See Mark 9:24 and John 6:37.

What Do You See?

1. What do the bowls and plates in this painting tell about Holy Communion?

2. Can you tell which disciple in the picture is Judas?

3. How does the presence of Judas at the Last Supper serve as a warning for us today?

The Holy Sacrament

Taking It Home

Spend 10 minutes or more discussing the following questions with your parent(s):

1. Describe a "nothing but the finest" meal your family celebrates. Why is it celebrated?
2. Talk about some of your family's prized heirlooms. How long have they been in the family? How did they end up in your home? Why are they so valuable to your family?
3. When has your "cup runneth over" with God's blessing?
4. How is celebrating Holy Communion like a family reunion?

Before the next session, review Questions 299–305 in *Luther's Small Catechism with Explanation.*

Divine Service

Key Verse

Oh give thanks to the Lord, *for He is good; for His steadfast love endures forever! Psalm 118:1*

Drama

After the Divine Service

(WADE and JOEL stand Center Stage. DAD is offstage. Each holds a Sunday bulletin.)

WADE: Well, Joel, what did you think?

JOEL: It was different.

WADE: Different, huh? What does that mean?

JOEL: I expected some of what we did. Some other things surprised me.

WADE: Like what?

JOEL: You sure sing a lot.

WADE: Yeah, I guess we do.

JOEL: And why did we keep standing up and sitting down? Sometimes I just wanted to stay sitting for a while.

WADE: I know what you mean. So what did you like?

JOEL: I liked the part where the pastor explained what is in the Bible. I understood what he meant. And I liked saying that prayer, the one that begins with "Our Father."

WADE: The Lord's Prayer.

JOEL: Right.

DAD: *(Enters Stage L)* Hey, guys.

WADE: Hi, Dad.

DAD: So how was church, Joel?

JOEL: I liked it a lot, Mr. Schultz.

WADE: Joel said he liked the sermon and the Lord's Prayer.

DAD: That's good. Can't go wrong with Pastor's sermons. And the Lord's Prayer, well, it's been around for two thousand years, and I don't know anyone who's tired of it.

WADE: What about all the singing, Dad? We were wondering why we sing so much.

DAD: I'm not really sure, but God's people have been singing for a very long time. The Book of Psalms in the Bible is a songbook for God's people. Maybe we've always sung just because we're so glad and so thankful. You know, sometimes you sing because you want to express what's deep inside.

JOEL: Did Jesus sing?

DAD: I think He did, Joel. Somewhere in the Bible it says that after Jesus and His disciples had celebrated the Lord's Supper, they sang a hymn.

WADE: One of those psalms, I bet.

DAD: Yeah, probably so.

JOEL: You know what I like about the Lord's Prayer, Mr. Schultz?

DAD: What's that?

JOEL: I liked how we kept saying "we" and "us" and "our." The prayer shows how we're in this together, doesn't it? It shows how we care about one another.

DAD: *(With a sense of wonder)* To be honest, Joel, I never thought about it that way. You're right, though. Good thought, buddy. I hope you come again next Sunday. Who knows, I may learn something! Now, let's get at those doughnuts. *(ALL begin to exit Stage R.)*

WADE: Say, Dad, about this standing up and sitting down . . .

DAD: "Holy aerobics," your grandpa calls it.

JOEL: "Holy aerobics"? *(All exit, laughing.)*

Discuss:

1. How would you describe the Divine Service to someone who rarely attends?
2. What did you think of Joel's understanding of the Lord's Prayer?
3. What does Joel's attending of the Divine Service tell you about Wade and his family?

Looking for Answers

1. What is the Divine Service?

2. Read the following portion of the introduction to *Lutheran Service Book*. Then answer the questions that follow.

Our Lord is the Lord who serves. Jesus Christ came into the flesh not to be served, but to serve and to give His life as a ransom for many. On the cross He offered Himself as a spotless sacrifice for the sin of the whole world. Through His perfect life and death, He accomplished forgiveness and salvation for all before the Father in heaven. By His empty tomb and ascension into heaven, He declared His victory over sin and death to all the world. Seated now at the Father's right hand, He graciously serves His Church with the gifts of salvation. On the Last Day, He will come again to gather His elect from every nation to celebrate the feast that will have no end.

Our Lord serves us today through His holy Word and Sacraments. Through these means, He comes among us to deliver His forgiveness and salvation, freeing us from our sins and strengthening us for service to one another and to the world. At Holy Baptism, He puts His name upon us, pours His Holy Spirit into our hearts, and rescues us from sin, death, and the devil. Through Holy Absolution, He pronounces His forgiveness again and again. With His holy Word, written in Scripture and preached into our ears, He daily proclaims His abiding love for us through all the joys and sorrows of life in this world. In His Holy Supper, He gives us His own body and blood to eat and drink as a priceless gift to nourish and strengthen us in both body and soul.

The Lord's service calls forth our service—in sacrifices of praise and thanksgiving to Him and in loving service to one another. Having been called, gathered, enlightened, and sanctified by the Holy Spirit, we receive His gifts with thankfulness and praise. With psalms, hymns, and spiritual songs, we joyfully confess all that God has done for us, declaring the praises of Him who called us out of darkness into His marvelous light. Our song joins with the song of every saint from every age, the new song of Christ's holy people, declaring: "Worthy is the Lamb who was slain, to receive power and wealth and wisdom and might and honor and glory and blessing!" (Rev. 5:12). (*LSB*, p. viii)

a. In what way did our God and Savior serve us in the past? In what way does He continue to serve His Church today? How will He serve His elect in the future?

b. Jesus comes to us today through His Word and the Sacraments. What blessings does He serve to us through these means?

c. How does Jesus serve us through Holy Baptism?

d. How does Jesus serve us through Holy Absolution?

e. How does Jesus serve us through His Holy Word?

f. How does Jesus serve us through His Holy Supper?

g. Describe the service to which our Lord's service calls us.

3. The following are components of the Divine Service. Draw an arrow pointing down if the Lord is speaking to us in this part of the service and an arrow pointing up if we are speaking or responding to Him. Some may have both up and down arrows. You may need to review these components of the Divine Service from the hymnal.

   Invocation:

   Confession and Absolution:

   Hymn of Praise:

   Readings:

   Hymn of the Day:

   Sermon:

   Creed:

   Prayers:

   Offerings:

   Preface to Communion:

   Lord's Prayer:

   Words of Institution:

   The Peace:

   Distribution:

   Prayer and Thanksgiving:

   Benediction:

4. How would you describe the rhythm of the Divine Service as you review the arrows pointing down and the arrows pointing up?

5. Why is it important that the hymns we sing first and foremost reflect God speaking to us?

6. Review the Lord's Supper liturgy. How do we prepare ourselves to receive the Supper? How do we respond to the blessings we receive in the Supper?

What Do We See?

1. What teaching is presented in this illustration?

2. Which of the benefits of the Lord's Supper remind us that Holy Communion resembles, in a way, a huge family meal?

3. What important teaching regarding what is received in the Sacrament is not directly presented in this illustration?

Receive the Benefits

Taking It Home

Spend 10 minutes or more discussing the following questions with your parent(s):

1. Whom could we invite to worship with us? When will we do it?

2. How important is it that the rhythm of worship focuses first on God speaking to us?

3. How important is it that the words we speak, hear, and sing in worship come from the Bible?

4. What are the most important things you have learned about yourself, God, and the Lord's Supper during the past weeks?